MARY WAGNER

NFLs Most Dominant Players

A List of the Top Players in Each Position

This book was professionally typeset on Reedsy.
Find out more at reedsy.com

"When you have great players, playing great, well that's great football!"

John Madden

Contents

1

Introduction

Welcome to the NFLs Most Dominant Players book. My name is Mary Wagner and I'm excited to be writing this book! I am going to give you a list of the most dominant NFL players at each position from a woman's point of view.

A little bit about myself...I am an avid football fan and have been watching it since I was a kid, be it local high school, major colleges on TV, and of course the NFL also on television. Being from the midwest you would think that my favorite team would be from nearby, but that is not the case. I had a favorite college player and when he got drafted, the team he went to became my team.

This book is my opinion and may not agree with other people's lists of who the most dominant player is at each position through the years. Some may be more recent players and others may be from longer ago.This is going to be based a lot on players that I watched playing. I may be a little biased to my team at times but I feel it is well deserved. So now, let's get started.

2

The Offense

This seems to be most everyone's favorite part of the team, as they are the side controlling the ball and scoring the points. Certain players on this side of the ball get a bulk of the attention from the media and fans, i.e. the quarterback, but they are doing most of the ball handling so it is with good reason that they get that attention. With that being said, here is the beginning of my list.

Quarterback

Yes, I am going to start with one of the most visible and favorite players on the team. There are a multitude of quarterbacks to choose from here. Some may think that Tom Brady is the most dominant. And that is a terrific choice. He is considered the G.O.A.T. or Greatest Of All Time, won 7 Super Bowls, and has the coveted most combined passing yards record. Others may think Aaron Rodgers, a 4 time league MVP, which is also a good one. Peyton Manning also deserves a mention here. But for me it's Joe Montana. He brought a very bad team into a dominant one in a short amount of time. He won all 4 Super Bowls he played in, of which he was MVP of 3 of them, and found ways to win even when the odds were against him which earned him the nickname "Joe Cool". He holds 3 NFL records being 2nd in playoff games with a passer rating over 100 with 12, most pass attempts without throwing an interception in a Super Bowl with 122, and most wins in a Super Bowl without a loss at 4 which he is tied with Terry Bradshaw. He was inducted into the Pro Football Hall of Fame in 2000.

Running Back

This was a tough one since there are so many great players to choose from. There was Barry Sanders and the late, great Walter Payton of which the NFL Man of the Year trophy is named after. There are current players Derrick Henry and Nick Chubbs that are making their mark right now. I am going to go with Emmitt Smith. He was small but effective at running the ball and helped Dallas win 3 Super Bowls in 4 years, 2 which were back to back, and earned the MVP in one of them. He still holds the NFL running record that Marcus Allen had at the time it was broken. He was the champion of season 2 Dancing with the Stars. He was inducted into the Pro Football Hall of Fame in 2010, along with Jerry Rice.

Full Back

I also have to give some attention to running backs that were not necessarily ball carriers but were used mostly for blocking. My choices for this are Tom Rathman for San Francisco and Daryl Johnston for Dallas, as they were so similar in what they did for their respective teams. Rathman blocked for the great running back Roger Craig and was a part of the West Coast offense of the 80s. He also did some rushing and catching of his own, helping San Francisco win 2 Super Bowls.

Johnston blocked for another great, Emmitt Smith, who he said was the key to his success at becoming the league's leading rusher. He retired due to a neck injury and moved to the broadcast booth as the color commentator for the NFL on FOX.

Wide Receiver

This is probably the second most liked player on the team and there are a lot to choose from. There was Tim Brown, Randy Moss, Michael Irvin, and the controversial Terrell Owens. But this is a no brainer and I think most everyone would agree with me that it is Jerry Rice. In the 15 seasons he played he broke every receiving record there was; career touchdown reception and receiving yards to name a couple. I believe he still holds a lot of those records even though he has not played for over 10 years. He was such a joy to watch and a pretty good dancer as well, coming in 2nd place on season 2 of Dancing with the Stars. He was inducted into the Pro Football Hall of Fame in 2010, along with Emmitt Smith.

Tight End

To me, tight ends have a different kind of mentality. They need to be tough for blocking but still be able to catch the ball. There are a couple of current tight ends that are blowing up the charts, along with their talent, namely George Kittle and Travis Kelce. But since they do not have a lot of games on their resume and are still in the prime of their playing careers, I went with someone else. Tony Gonzales is the model that most tight ends should follow. He was durable and known for not being a fumbler. Improvements could be seen with each new season which is a testament to his work ethic. He eventually broke the career touchdown reception record for tight ends which had been held by Shannon Sharpe. Many consider him the greatest tight end of all time and I would tend to agree. He was inducted into the Pro Football Hall of Fame in 2019.

The other is most recent retiree Rob Gronkowski. He won 4 Super Bowls overall, 3 with New England and 1 with Tampa Bay. He was very versatile and very good at blocking and receiving. Once he caught the ball it was often difficult to tackle him before he gained a lot of yards. He is known for his "Gronk Spike". He retired in 2019 but came back and played 2 more seasons before retiring again in 2022.

Offensive Line

Last but certainly not least is the offensive line. The big guys in the trenches; protecting the quarterback; making holes for the running back. I have to admit that these are players that many did not become household names, so I am going to name players that I am familiar with.

Center

The center is the second player that handles the ball the most as he is the one hiking it to the quarterback. I have to admit I am not familiar with some of the names on the top 10 list of greatest centers. For this I am going to choose Randy Cross. He hiked the ball to both Joe Montana and Steve Young so why not pick him? He spent his whole 13 year career with San Francisco, winning 3 Super Bowls. He retired after their Super Bowl XXIII win and turned to broadcasting as an analyst for CBS Sports and later for NBC Sports.

Guards

Again, there are a lot of players for this position that I am not that familiar with so I am going with the ones I remember. Since there is a right one and left one, there will be 2 in this category.

First, I'm going with Guy McIntyre, blocking for future Hall of Famers Joe Montana and Steve Young. He was a 3 time Super Bowl champion and was one of the first linemen to be used as a blocking back instead of his traditional position. Because of this idea, Chicago used William "The Refrigerator" Perry in the same way.

Second is Randall McDaniel. He spent most of his career with Minnesota in which he played in 202 consecutive games. From 1989 - 2000 he started in 12 Pro Bowls, which ties a record for most played. He was inducted into the Pro Football Hall of Fame in 2009.

Tackles

These are the players that, depending on which hand the quarterback was throwing from, were protecting his blind side, stopping a blitz, or a bull rush from a quick linebacker. Again, there is a right one and a left one so I chose 2.

First is Anthony Munoz. Once he became a starter he remained to be an integral part of the offensive line which included 2 Super Bowls, both being losses to San Francisco. He was Offensive Lineman of the Year for the NFL twice and the NFL Players Association and NFL Alumni Association 4 times each. He was inducted into the Pro Football Hall of Fame in 1998.

Second, I am going with Orlando Pace. He primarily played for the then St. Louis Rams and was the first overall draft pick in 1997. In 2000 he was part of a trio of Rams' linemen not to have been penalized for holding. He was a blocker for the NFL MVP in 3 straight years, Kurt Warner in 1999 and 2001 and Marshall Faulk in 2000. He was inducted into the Pro Football Hall of Fame in 2016.

3

The Defense

I have heard it said that offense wins games but that defense wins championships. Defense is about working hard to stop the opposing teams' offense so that their offense can get back on the field to score. So, these defensive players are an integral part of the team. Here are my choices.

Linebackers

Depending on the defensive set, there could be a different number of inside and outside linebackers. In the 4-3 defense there is 1 inside or middle linebacker and 2 outside linebackers. In the 3-4 defense there are 2 inside linebackers and 2 outside linebackers.

I am going to start with middle linebacker since there is only 1 in the 4-3 defense and none in the other. There are a multitude of very talented players but the one that stood for me was Ray Lewis. He was always trying to motivate his team during a game with encouragement and his entrance dance was one of the best ones in my opinion. In 2000 he was on a record setting defense that led to winning the Super Bowl and becoming the MVP. In his final season playing he tore his triceps and came back to finish the season and playoffs with a Super Bowl win. He also played the inside linebacker when it was the 3-4 defense, so I chose him for 1 of those as well. When he retired he became a broadcaster for ESPN. He was inducted into the Pro Football Hall of Fame in 2018.

Another dominant inside linebacker was Brian Urlacher. He was considered the most talented prospect of the 2000 draft. He started in 180 of the 182 games that he played in over his career. After he retired he appeared in several commercials and was on Wheel of Fortune, which he won over $47,000 for his charity. He was inducted into the Pro Football Hall of Fame in 2018.

The outside linebackers played in either defensive set so I am choosing 2 for this position. Lawrence Taylor, also known as L.T., is the overwhelming first choice for me. In a quote from the late John Madden, he said "Lawrence Taylor, defensively, has had as big an impact as any player I've ever seen. He changed the way defense is played, the way pass-rushing is played, the way linebackers play and the way offenses block linebackers." Some coaches changed the way they blocked when they played against him to slow him down, but at times to no avail. He was inducted into the Pro Football Hall of Fame in 1999.

The other outside linebacker that I am choosing is Derrick Brooks. He had the speed, agility, and instinct on where to be on certain plays. In his 14 year career with Tampa Bay, he started in 221 of 224 games. In 2002 he was named the NFL's Defensive Player of the Year and helped win the teams' first ever Super Bowl. He also went into broadcasting for ESPN. He was inducted into the Pro Football Hall of Fame in 2014.

Corner backs

This is one of the toughest positions to play by having to cover the fastest players on the opposing team and try to anticipate their routes. They seem to be one of the most vital players on every Super Bowl team. I am picking Deion Sanders as one of the 2 corner backs. He may be considered one of the greatest corner backs of all time. He also played baseball part time for 4 different teams with the seasons crossing over each other. He has an impressive resume. To name a few he was the only man to play in both the Super Bowl and World Series; the only player to hit a major league home run and score a touchdown in the same week; be selected to the Pro Bowl for 3 different positions: corner back, safety and kick returner. Whew, that is quite a list and that is just scratching the surface. He was inducted into the Pro Football Hall of Fame in 2009.

The other would have to be Ronnie Lott. As a rookie, he showed skill in training camp that garnered him the starting job. After the season in 1985 he had the tip of his left pinkie finger amputated when it got crushed while tackling a running back. He played 10 years for San Francisco helping them to win 8 division titles and 4 Super Bowls. He was inducted into the Pro Football Hall of Fame in 2000.

Safeties

These players have a lot of responsibilities. Covering the long ball and being a factor against the run being the top ones. Ronnie Lott is also on this list for me as he switched to the position during his career.

The other one I like is John Lynch. He began his playing career on special teams and eventually moved to safety. He was on the 2002 Tampa Bay team that won the Super Bowl. After he retired, he was a broadcaster for the NFL on FOX. He has been inducted into both Tampa Bay's and Denver's Ring of Honor in the same year. In 2017 he was named the General Manager for San Francisco. He was inducted into the Pro Football Hall of Fame in 2021.

Defensive Ends

Rushing the passer is the most important responsibility of the defensive end. They can either sack the quarterback, force a fumble, or cause an ill advised pass that could lead to an interception. My first choice is of course "The Minister of Defense'', Reggie White. He was Defensive Player of the year but more valued as a team leader. His only Super Bowl championship was with Green Bay but it was memorable. He had 10 sacks a game for 9 consecutive years, which is a record. After retiring, Reggie focused on his Christian ministry. He was posthumously inducted into the Pro Football Hall of Fame in 2006.

My second choice is Howie Long. He played all 13 years of his career in Oakland, winning numerous awards, and Super Bowl XVIII. At the time that he retired, he was the last player still with the team who had been a Raider before the franchise moved to Los Angeles. After retirement he did some acting, pursuing action films. He eventually moved to broadcasting where he is currently in the role as studio analyst for the pregame show on FOX since 1994. He was inducted into the Pro Football Hall of Fame in 2000.

Defensive Tackles

I am going with a couple with some flair and personality. With that being said I first choose Warren Sapp. He had the combination of size and speed which was difficult to block even when double and triple teamed and was a prolific tackler. He was part of the "Tampa 2" defense which included Derrick Brooks and John Lynch. He had some on field altercations as well as off field legal issues. He was on Dancing with the Stars on season 7 in which he came in second place. He was inducted into the Pro Football Hall of Fame in 2013.

My second choice is John Randle. He was undrafted and eventually signed with Minnesota on a recommendation of the head scout. It turned out to be an excellent choice as he became one of the most dominant tackles in the NFL. Brett Favre of division rival Green Bay was the quarterback he sacked the most. Favre said that he was the most difficult player he faced and that he was "unblockable". He was inducted into the Pro Football Hall of Fame in 2010 along with Jerry Rice and Emmitt Smith.

4

Special Teams

Special teams are players that are involved in kicking plays, such as kick offs, punts, and extra points. They can dictate how a game may go for instance if a kick or punt is returned for a touchdown, or a blocked punt. It can be a make or break moment for a team. There are different teams, depending on the situation. There are the Kickoff Team, Kick Return Team, Punt Team, Punt Return Team, Field Goal / Extra Point Team, Field Goal Block Team, Extra Point Team, Extra Point Block Team, and The Hands Team. The positions on these teams are Kicker, Punter, Holder, Long Snapper, Kick Returner, Punt Returner, Gunner, and Personal Protector. Most of these players are not playing a lot on offense or defense, so they contribute to these teams. The only player that does not participate on special teams is the starting quarterback, and for good reason. I am only going to touch on the specific positions that are the integral part of special teams. Here are my picks for the different positions.

Kicker

This player kicks extra points and field goals. They usually kick off unless the punter has a stronger leg. They are the most important players on special teams and usually the leading scorers on the team. This was a toss up for me between Adam Vinatieri and Justin Tucker, but I am going with the former.

Vinatieri played a very important part in many of New England's wins including 4 Super Bowls. He is the all time leading scorer in the NFL. The 365 games he played is second to Morten Andersen's 382. He holds many other records including most field goals made which was 599 and most consecutive seasons scoring of 24. He retired in May, 2021.

Punter

This player punts and may sometimes be the holder for field goals. Their job is to pin the opposing team deep in their territory. Field position, especially in a low scoring defensive struggle, could mean a win or a loss. My choice is Ray Guy. He played his entire career with the Raiders. In his early years he was the emergency quarterback for kicker/quarterback George Blanda. He also did some kickoffs when the aging Blanda could not kick the ball deep any more. He was more known for kicking the ball very high than for distance. By the time the ball would come down the coverage team had the field covered so that there was little or no chance of any return yardage. He was finally inducted into the Pro Football Hall of Fame in 2014.

Kick Returner

There is not a play any more exciting, other than a game winning Hail Mary, than a kickoff that is returned for a touchdown. Since a rule change a few years ago made for the safety of the players, many of today's kick offs result in a touch back. But when there was a kickoff return it could sometimes dictate the momentum and possible outcome of the game. It is a beautiful thing to see as a spectator when you see the blocking open up the field and the returner hitting those holes just right to go all the way.

For this position I am going to go with Joshua Cribbs. He holds many Cleveland franchise records including most career kickoff return yards of 10,015 and most career combined kickoff and punt return touchdowns of 11. He is tied for 3 NFL records which are 8 most career kickoff return touchdowns, 2 kickoff return touchdowns of 100 yards or more in a single game, and 2 most kickoff return touchdowns in a single game. He retired in 2017.

Punt Returner

This player needs to be fast and shifty. They should have the vision to see possible openings in the coverage and the quick decision making to go for it or not.

For me it is Devin Hester. He is considered the greatest return specialist in NFL history. During his career he was the most feared returner. Most kickers would kick the ball away from him to prevent a possible return for a touchdown. He holds the record for most non-offensive touchdowns at 20 (that also includes kickoff returns). He also has the fastest touchdown in Super Bowl history at 14 seconds. He retired in 2017.

5

Conclusion

There it is. The most dominant NFL players at each position in my opinion. I hope you enjoyed the book and maybe found out some things you didn't know about some of the players.

If you found this book entertaining, I would be most appreciative if you would leave a favorable review on Amazon.

6

Resources

McVey, R. (2022b, April 8). 25 Greatest Quarterbacks in NFL History. AthlonSports.Com | Expert Predictions, Picks, and Previews. Retrieved August 13, 2022, from https://athlonsports.com/nfl/25-greatest-quarterbacks-nfl-history-2016

Wikipedia contributors. (2022, August 9). Joe Montana. Wikipedia. Retrieved August 13, 2022, from https://en.wikipedia.org/wiki/Joe_Montana

McVey, R. (2022c, April 16). 25 Greatest Running Backs in NFL History. AthlonSports.Com | Expert Predictions, Picks, and Previews. Retrieved August 13, 2022, from https://athlonsports.com/nfl/25-greatest-running-backs-nfl-history

Wikipedia contributors. (2002, December 5). Emmitt Smith. Wikipedia. Retrieved August 13, 2022, from https://en.wikipedia.org/wiki/Emmitt_Smith

Wikipedia contributors. (2022a, May 5). Tom Rathman. Wikipedia.

Retrieved August 13, 2022, from https://en.wikipedia.org/wiki/Tom_Rathman

Wikipedia contributors. (2022b, June 25). Daryl Johnston. Wikipedia. Retrieved August 13, 2022, from https://en.wikipedia.org/wiki/Daryl_Johnston

Tallent, A. (2022, February 18). 25 Greatest Wide Receivers in NFL History. AthlonSports.Com | Expert Predictions, Picks, and Previews. Retrieved August 13, 2022, from https://athlonsports.com/nfl/25-greatest-wide-receivers-nfl-history

Wikipedia contributors. (2022c, July 17). Jerry Rice. Wikipedia. Retrieved August 13, 2022, from https://en.wikipedia.org/wiki/Jerry_Rice

Scott, J. P. (2022, June 22). 25 Greatest Tight Ends in NFL History. AthlonSports.Com | Expert Predictions, Picks, and Previews. Retrieved August 13, 2022, from https://athlonsports.com/nfl/25-greatest-tight-ends-nfl-history

Wikipedia contributors. (2022e, August 10). Tony Gonzalez. Wikipedia. Retrieved August 13, 2022, from https://en.wikipedia.org/wiki/Tony_Gonzalez

Wikipedia contributors. (2009, April 30). Rob Gronkowski. Wikipedia. Retrieved August 13, 2022, from https://en.wikipedia.org/wiki/Rob_Gronkowski

Brandt, G. (2020, May 7). Gil Brandt's greatest NFL centers of all time. NFL.Com. Retrieved August 13, 2022, from https://www.nfl.com/photos/gil-brandt-s-greatest-nfl-centers-of-all-time-0ap3000000816749

Wikipedia contributors. (2022e, August 10). Randy Cross. Wikipedia. Retrieved August 13, 2022, from https://en.wikipedia.org/wiki/Randy_ Cross

Brandt, G. (2020c, May 7). Gil Brandt's greatest NFL guards of all time. NFL.Com. Retrieved August 13, 2022, from https://www.nfl.com/photos /gil-brandt-s-greatest-nfl-guards-of-all-time-0ap3000000816668

Wikipedia contributors. (2022b, May 11). Guy McIntyre. Wikipedia. Retrieved August 13, 2022, from https://en.wikipedia.org/wiki/Guy_ McIntyre

Wikipedia contributors. (2022a, April 6). Randall McDaniel. Wikipedia. Retrieved August 13, 2022, from https://en.wikipedia.org/wiki/Randall _McDaniel

Brandt, G. (2020e, May 7). Gil Brandt's greatest NFL tackles of all time. NFL.Com. Retrieved August 13, 2022, from https://www.nfl.com/photos /gil-brandt-s-greatest-nfl-tackles-of-all-time-0ap3000000816586

Wikipedia contributors. (2022f, August 6). Anthony Muñoz. Wikipedia. Retrieved August 13, 2022, from https://en.wikipedia.org/wiki/Anthon y_Mu%C3%B1oz

Wikipedia contributors. (2022e, July 11). Orlando Pace. Wikipedia. Retrieved August 13, 2022, from https://en.wikipedia.org/wiki/Orlan do_Pace

McVey, R. (2022, February 18). 25 Greatest Linebackers in NFL History. AthlonSports.Com | Expert Predictions, Picks, and Previews. Retrieved August 13, 2022, from https://athlonsports.com/nfl/25-greatest-lineb

ackers-nfl-history

Wikipedia contributors. (2022g, August 3). Ray Lewis. Wikipedia. Retrieved August 13, 2022, from https://en.wikipedia.org/wiki/Ray_ Lewis

Wikipedia contributors. (2022m, August 13). Brian Urlacher. Wikipedia. Retrieved August 13, 2022, from https://en.wikipedia.org/wiki/Brian_ Urlacher

Bofah, K. (2017, April 8). NFL: The 10 Greatest Cornerbacks of All Time. Sportscasting | Pure Sports. Retrieved August 13, 2022, from https://ww w.sportscasting.com/top-10-greatest-nfl-cornerbacks-of-all-time-2/

Wikipedia contributors. (2022n, August 13). Deion Sanders. Wikipedia. Retrieved August 13, 2022, from https://en.wikipedia.org/wiki/Deion_ Sanders

Wikipedia contributors. (2022i, August 7). Ronnie Lott. Wikipedia. Retrieved August 13, 2022, from https://en.wikipedia.org/wiki/Ronnie_ Lott

Brandt, G. (2020d, May 7). Gil Brandt's greatest NFL safeties of all time. NFL.Com. Retrieved August 13, 2022, from https://www.nfl.com/phot os/gil-brandt-s-greatest-nfl-safeties-of-all-time-0ap30000008162 54

Wikipedia contributors. (2022g, August 2). John Lynch (American football). Wikipedia. Retrieved August 13, 2022, from https://en.wik ipedia.org/wiki/John_Lynch_(American_football)

Brandt, G. (2020, May 7). Gil Brandt's greatest defensive ends of all time. NFL.Com. Retrieved August 14, 2022, from https://www.nfl.com/photos/gil-brandt-s-greatest-defensive-ends-of-all-time-0ap3000000815984

Wikipedia contributors. (2022n, August 11). Reggie White. Wikipedia. Retrieved August 14, 2022, from https://en.wikipedia.org/wiki/Reggie_White

Wikipedia contributors. (2022s, August 14). Howie Long. Wikipedia. Retrieved August 14, 2022, from https://en.wikipedia.org/wiki/Howie_Long

Brandt, G. (2020b, May 20). Gil Brandt's greatest NFL defensive tackles of all time. NFL.Com. Retrieved August 14, 2022, from https://www.nfl.com/photos/gil-brandt-s-greatest-nfl-defensive-tackles-of-all-time-0ap3000000816301

Wikipedia contributors. (2022o, August 11). Warren Sapp. Wikipedia. Retrieved August 14, 2022, from https://en.wikipedia.org/wiki/Warren_Sapp

Wikipedia contributors. (2022e, July 9). John Randle. Wikipedia. Retrieved August 14, 2022, from https://en.wikipedia.org/wiki/John_Randle

Dockett, E. (2022, April 20). NFL Football Special Teams Explained. HowTheyPlay. Retrieved August 13, 2022, from https://howtheyplay.com/team-sports/NFL-Football-Special-Teams-Explained

Scott, J. P. (2022, February 18). 10 Greatest Kickers in NFL History. AthlonSports.Com | Expert Predictions, Picks, and Previews. Retrieved

August 14, 2022, from https://athlonsports.com/nfl/10-greatest-kicke rs-nfl-history

Wikipedia contributors. (2022f, August 14). Adam Vinatieri. Wikipedia. Retrieved August 14, 2022, from https://en.wikipedia.org/wiki/Adam_ Vinatieri

Brandt, G. (2020b, May 7). Gil Brandt's greatest NFL punters of all time. NFL.Com. Retrieved August 14, 2022, from https://www.nfl.com/photos /gil-brandt-s-greatest-nfl-punters-of-all-time-0ap3000000817839

Wikipedia contributors. (2022d, June 8). Ray Guy. Wikipedia. Retrieved August 14, 2022, from https://en.wikipedia.org/wiki/Ray_Guy

Maggio, A. (2015, January 2). Top 15 Kick Returners of All Time. The Sportster. Retrieved August 14, 2022, from https://www.thesportster.c om/football/top-15-kick-returners-of-all-time/

Bennellick, R. (2022, July 23). NFL: Who is the best punt/kick returner in league history? Sportskeeda. Retrieved August 14, 2022, from https://w ww.sportskeeda.com/nfl/nfl-who-best-punt-kick-returner-nfl-hist ory

Wikipedia contributors. (2022l, August 7). Josh Cribbs. Wikipedia. Retrieved August 14, 2022, from https://en.wikipedia.org/wiki/Josh_ Cribbs

Wikipedia contributors. (2022m, August 8). Devin Hester. Wikipedia. Retrieved August 14, 2022, from https://en.wikipedia.org/wiki/Devin_ Hester